# *Cut On The Bias*

**Julie Boden**

**Pontefract Press**

Publisher:              Pontefract Press
17 Linden Terrace
Pontefract
WF8 4AE
Telephone: 01977 793121


©                     Text: Julie Boden


Cover design:    Harry Malkin
Book design:    Reini Schuhle and Brian Lewis, Pontefract Press


Publication date:  Summer 2002
Reprinted       2007

ISBN:            1 900325 29 2

*For Nathaniel and Charlotte*

# *Preface*

The poems in *Cut on the Bias* are crafted and very often, in the best sense of the phrase, made from 'found' materials. Birmingham and the Midlands loom large; one of the meanings we might take from the title refers to the canals that have been cut through the rural and industrial Midlands. There is affection for the landscape; echoes of the poet Roy Fisher's love for Birmingham perhaps. Spaghetti Junction, the Cross City Line, Sutton Coldfield, the City Centre, become a litany capable of resonating for natives and strangers alike. All is not good - by no means - but it is real and mostly unsung. This is not the North or the Celtic fringe, heavy with association, but it is somewhere that has a particular flavour and is so often misrepresented.

The landscape is also its people and it is good that so many of the poems focus on the lives of various types of every-man and every-woman. It is so refreshing to read so many poems that do not include the first person pronoun. Not that the author's voice is absent, but it is showing not telling, keeping a studied neutrality, holding something back. There is a pleasing cynicism too that ripples through the poems and also an understanding of how frail the human heart can be and how weak the flesh. Which brings us to the second meaning we might take from the title - the dress or skirt cut from cloth at an angle for appearance's sake to make the wearer look better than they are or at least to allow them to believe this to be so. The world is a dissembling place and we cannot trust the way things look. We cannot even trust ourselves.

What links the many subjects of these poems is a real desire to let form and content work in support of each other. Formal structures, rhyme schemes, stress counts, even perhaps the typographical look of the poems, are used in a deliberate and refreshing way. Form enriches content, draws it out from itself, slightly separates it from its source, mesmerises us and makes it a thing of art. This brings us, finally, to the writer - and often performer - of these poems. Julie Boden is clearly one of those writers who actually wants to write, who takes a pleasure in writing, who is not precious with her work or reverential about herself, but who wants to communicate as clearly as possible to her readers and listeners and fellow performers. There is hard graft and inspiration behind these poems but also, and most importantly, a love of the language, its sound and meaning, its possibilities and limits.

*Jonathan Davidson*

# CONTENTS

## Birmingham Rhapsody

Of man's own rising from this city's sleep,
of avenues of trees, where conker falls
may bring on death and council tales of woe,
a loss of seat; the hope of greater Man
restore us, let the Bullring rise again.
Sing, 'Flying Eye' that over Birmingham
does whirl to tell commuters travel news,
take from my head its lid and pull one thread,
rotate it in an anti-clockwise way,
invoke your aid to my advent'rous song
that with no middle flight intends to show
the seven Brummie hills in prose and rhyme:
the Chaos and heroic Pantomime.


\*\*\*


'Lift not your fist against the Hyatt Tower,'
a registry shines from Symphony Hall,
the culture of Spaghetti Junction's true:
spaghetti roads and straight canals
all find their own way through.


\*\*\*


A Jerk in a Merc
hits another red light
slams his brakes so hard
that his lap-top takes flight.

He phones another Jerk up
on his mobile phone,
bangs his steering wheel in anger,
clips another traffic cone.

Portia in the Porsche
has a car that sings her name.
Dearest daddy bought it for her,
Darling daddy is to blame
for the attitude that takes her
down from Oxford to the bar.
Watch her blow a kiss to daddy.
Man, this girl is going far.

The man in the van
doesn't know what to do.
The sexy beast he married
is the old bag in the shoe.
He tells his mate his troubles
and his mate says, 'It's oriyt.
She's exploded. We'll get loaded.
Let's go on the piss tonight.'

A woman winds her window down.
She's pretty, young and fair.
When the traffic's at a standstill
she begins to brush her hair.
She is putting on her lipstick,
she is putting on mascara,
she is looking in the mirror
for the eyes of an admirer.

\*\*\*

And under the roads
on the rails of a track
there's a city,
cross-city,
a city attack.
They're crammed
in compartments,
speeding along.
They wish
they could fish
but the train moves along.
No time to dream,
no time to lose.
They'll never
score goals
for the Villa
or Blues.
Journey to work,
ticket back home,
Metro, Big Issue,
a journey alone.
Ignoble strife
back to the wife,
the kids and the
mortgage,
to New Street
and life.

\*\*\*

Above their heads, 'Star City' thinks itself Titanic
riding the roofs that fall back on the crests of themselves.

\*\*\*

This is a city of legends and myths, unsaid.
From cracks in the concrete, the wails of the dead
are calling for justice and crying in vain
as a wind steals their voices before Steelhouse Lane.

*\*\**

Here lies Jane. Here lies John.
In the pillars you fly on.
This Underworld; a gangster's gaff:
this is their future epitaph.

*\*\**

See the Smartie car
spring, Haiku, around pillar
leading a Renga.

*\*\**

Far from the taste of Cadbury World
a voice recalls our city's name.
One afternoon of heat,
a concrete collar drove them round it,
round and round and round again.
They've heard it's gone,
the city's changed,
the sign posts have been rearranged.
One day they'll come again.

*\*\**

Londoners know all too well,
one only shows, one does not tell,
the secret of artistic notion
is the singular thread
in the circular motion.

\*\*\*

It's Spag Bog 'n' Balti down Birmingham way.
The junction tuxedos have outgrown their day.
BEAST feeds its sound to the ears of its prey
as steel bands and orchestra take it away.
No harm in the harmonic cultures we play.
Diversity-Versity, verse city, hey…

We'll wing it,
let's sing it,
we'll swing it and say…

'We're jamming the Brumagen way.'

### Cross City Line

A set of Sutton Coldfield stalagmites
are standing in a sharp surreal air

beneath the uniform of grey/black coats
hold holidays of sun and sand and sex.

A young girl with a pony tail scraped back
knows the soreness of a stud that no one sees.

The morning wooden platform marks no squares
but all these crow commuters know their place.

Strange chess statues guard their bits of ground,
standing on the opening of day,

when they hear the whistle of the train
they step a Stepford foot onto a step,

cloak their dreams in cashmere Klingon coats,
raise their FT/ Metro forcefields up,

show the world a book they never read
but like to think that others think they have.

Before the chess clock push of day begins
these rook brains plan the castling of kings.

### Memories in a City Café

This tale tells of a café and a song:
a man who tried but could not understand
how life could grow so sad and stretch so long.
He held the round green table in his hand,
its yellow rim rang out a silent wrong.
This end was not the fairytale he'd planned.

Where were the dreams his yesterdays had planned?
In youth, in joy, the slow dance was their song.
When she grew old he thought she'd understand.
As days grew short and memories grew long
he'd hoped that she would hold his livered hand,
but she could only point out what went wrong.

'To be quite frank,' she snapped, 'you did me wrong,
the summer of the heat wave that you planned
the smart seduction scene, the fevered song.
I was naïve and did not understand
the passions of a man who waits too long
and now I have this yoke upon my hand.'

Through all the years he did not raise a hand.
He would not argue, tell her she was wrong.
He went along with everything she planned,
however strange the key, he sang her song.
He always listened, tried to understand
while she screamed accusations all night long.

The days and nights, the weeks and months grew long
her fingers spread, the ring cut in her hand.
As he put right the things that were not wrong
she blamed the stars, the signs that plotted, planned,
the wind, the rain, the sun, the birds, the song,
a harmony she could not understand.

But he has always tried to understand.
He comes here now to rest when days grow long,
to feel the yellow rim beneath his hand.
He writes the shopping list that will be wrong.
She'll tell him his forgetfulness was planned
then shout at him for humming some sad song.

It was their song. She does not understand,
for far too long he'd hoped she'd hold his hand,
admit for once, 'My love, I'm wrong, so wrong…
to go on so…' - that's all that he had planned.

## Tesco 911

Why did she have to spoil their Friday night?
He liked it when his mum went to the shops.
His dad played aeroplanes with bits of food
And sometimes let him taste the halal chops.

His mouth became a runway for the night
as Dad became a jet, a plane with props.
Why couldn't this be like all other nights?
Why did she have to drag them to the shops?

Why must they go to Tesco's for their tea?
His Lego called him back to build new towers.
Shopping's boring, stupid; shops are hot.
Why did they have to buy his mum some flowers?

They counted out the ways. Dad said, 'Five days.
It's only been five days, son. Give it time.'
His dad was acting weird, so was his mum.
they whispered him to bed, they talked in mime.

His mother's hair was shining in the sun
He asked her if her scarf had fallen off.
She smiled, then looked away, but didn't say.
His dad just cleared his throat; a nervous cough.

His mother didn't want to shop alone,
she needed her two men to help her through.
His father said, 'Your eyes are your best veil,'
and in her eyes she said, 'How true, how true.'

## *Loading the Glass Washer*

We serve up food to eat. We're raving mad.
When on the telly, faces are so tragic,
How can they breathe? The world is just too sad.
My horror-scope says now's the time for magic.

When on the telly, faces are so tragic,
I just can't bear to watch 'em most the time.
My horror-scope says now's the time for magic.
I see the angels come when till bells chime.

I just can't bear to watch 'em most the time:
the people who come in and out of 'ere.
I see the angels come when till bells chime,
behind this bar that's where they all appear.

The people who come in and out of 'ere
they are a funny bunch, it must be said.
Behind this bar, that's where they all appear
with boaters just like 'ayloes on  their 'ead.

They are a funny bunch, it must be said.
We serve up food to eat. We're raving mad.
With boaters just like 'ayloes on  their 'ead.
How can they breathe? The world is just too sad.

### Balkans, Belfast, Bethlehem

I'm sick of politicians and their party polytricks.
*Balkans, Belfast, Bethlehem*

The blood suck of the insects' parasitic polyticks.
*Balkans, Belfast, Bethlehem*

The camera calls of RADA smiles that say, 'Truth shall Deliver.'
The sly lip-slipping men in suits who sell us down the river.
*Balkans, Belfast, Bethlehem*

It's the big and little endians who pow-wow at the table
who argue where to crack the egg then stick us with a label.
On the branches of our tree the small twigs snap an angry blame.
Can't they Adam and believe the fact our roots are all the same?

It's not some daft naïve belief, it's there in books of Science,
so can't we face the future in a spirit of alliance?
The snapping twigs have always tried to scream away their pain.
From an Adam and an Eve, there came an Abel and a Cain.

*Balkans, Belfast, Bethlehem*

### God Wanted Dead or Alive

Have you seen all the new wanted posters
that are plastered all over the place?
The letters are bold,
but words seem so cold
when they hold out a big empty space.

They've taken up pencils to draw him.
They draw. They draw out. They erase.
For no one is clear
just what picture goes here.
No one knows or remembers his face.

I think God has found an allotment
where he turns over soil at a pace.
Be it war or Jihad
the world has gone mad
and he's sick of the whole human race.

## Cut on the Bias

King Edward's Wharf in Ladywood invites the city set
to a life cut on the bias where the water's not too wet.
You can wander off to Broad Street, live a lifetime of regret,
then recover in a Halcyon of days.

Where statues made by Quinn are hidden in a courtyard square
there's an egg they call 'Creation', there's a wheel that cries despair
and a gallery of angels view the life sized sculptures there.
In this courtyard, there's a Halcyon of days.

An egg set on a pyramid is caught inside a square.
There's a man whose arms would fly out of his treadmill of despair
and a workman in a hard hat eats his sandwiches just there
where a courtyard breathes a Halcyon of days.

But the man beneath the hard hat finds he cannot scratch his head
when he sees a vase of Willow, he is sad that wood is dead,
how he'd love to dig the garden up, plant fruit and veg instead
from his labour, grow a Halcyon of days.

If the concierge should see me, I am sure he'd think I'm odd
for I'm talking to Quinn's statues as they hide inside the Quad
quoting limericks on Berkeley, can't help wondering if God
has a hand that holds a Halcyon of days.

## Café Rouge

Outside window walk the men in suits.
Man wipes mouth with finger then phones home,
stands inside the doorway, enters café,
talks at wife in disconnected tone.
One quick finger flick turns off his phone.

Peroxide smiling broiler enters scene,
lipstick-pecks the grey man's rich cheekbone.
Waiter sidles up, slides them to seats.
He turns to leave, then hears a siren moan
calling from the dark secluded zone.

Her handbag, apple coloured, promise bright
holds screwed up brochure sights of nights in Rome.
Crème fraiche glacée cools his forking tongue.
His table sharer whispers, 'Come tonight,
you know I need to have you on your own.'

Beneath the Alpha Tower he lifts her skirt.
They prise themselves apart; walk home alone.
Through T-shirt night, in omega of suit
he rubs his lips and reconnects his phone,
talks to wife in disconnected tone.

## Metro Motion

*Snippety snap, snippety snap,*
*this is the way they begin the attack.*
*Snippety snap, snappety snap,*
*snippety, snappety, snappety snap.*

> They catch the moment out in sliding doors,
> hum a lullaby that sings their pram
> split the second, not the atom here,
> quantum leap their bodies on a tram.

*Riding the beam, flying the track,*
*speeding to work like a borg in a pack.*
*Trickety track, treckety track,*
*trickety, treckety, trackety track.*

> The student and the teacher and the nurse
> the seller and the buyer and the clerk
> rhyme a multiverse of hopes and dreams
> sabre shine their light beams in the dark.

*Snippety snap, snickety snack,*
*into the city, a city attack.*
*Snippety snap, snackety snack,*
*Snippety, snappety, snackety snack.*

> Trapped inside the armour of their suits
> looping in the vinyl of a track
> playing and replaying special songs
> that the rhythm of a carriage carries back.

*Rock of a pram, shock of a pram*
*trapped in a tube, in a tube of a tram.*
*Mush of a tram, crush of a tram*
*rush of a, mush of a, crush of a tram.*

Climbing e-mail mountains every morning
pushing random paper round and round
they grab a snack, snatch coffee, guzzle crisps
then push another heap of paper round.

*Snickety snack, snackety snack*
*no time to sit it's a sandwich attack.*
*Snippety snack, snackety snack*
*working and eating. No time to snack.*

As they walk and talk they type in text:
2b or not 2b. Wassup. Wassat.
Punctuate their days with digit speak:
c u 7 (smiley face) on Sat.

*Riding the beam, flying the track,*
*speeding to work and then slip sliding back.*
*Bleakely back, blankely back,*
*Bleakely, blinckety, blankely back.*

5 o' clock the metro-gnomes are moving
creeping through their solitude in space.
As dusk spits night, splits light, slowly moving
the metro-gnomes are giving up the race.

### *The Lady in Red*


The lady in red wears an haute couture dress
it's cut on the bias to move as she walks,
with Harvey Nick's label and Royal Arch address
the lady in red wears an haute couture dress.
She travels first class, always goes by express,
she's pure Valentino, she sings as she talks.
The Lady in red wears an haute couture dress
it's cut on the bias to move as she walks.

## Essentials

Her handbag's not a handbag, it's a skip.
I'm told it's something snails can understand.
She needs to keep her family to hand,
to swing a shell of home against her hip.

For every problem there's a useful tip,
all odd jobs can be fixed, she has them canned.
Her handbag's not a handbag, it's a skip.
I'm told it's something snails can understand.

Each day's a Winnebago-teepee trip.
They only stand and wait who wait and stand,
but she, who does not wait, she has it planned:

spare knickers, kitchen sink and paper clip,
her handbag's not a handbag, it's a skip.
I'm told it's something snails can understand.

## *Atonement*

'e didn't mean to do 'er any arm.
The poor kid only 'ad 'n ancient phone.
'is friends all said it 'ad a borin' tone
when from 'er bag, there came a cool alarm.

They've found a way to 'elp the lad 'atone',
'e does 'community' at City Farm.
'e didn't mean to do 'er any arm.
The poor kid only 'ad 'n ancient phone.

'is mother is on Prozac, she's quite calm.
It's just their luck his victim broke an arm,
or two; a leg. His dad left them alone.

It's not their fault. 'e 'as is father's charm.
'e didn't mean to do 'er any 'arm.
The poor kid only 'ad 'n ancient phone.

## Card from the Coffee Republic

The city council strung their logo up in lights.
Season's Greetings hang above the road.
I sit at the Republic, raise a cup to friends,
watch little donkeys heave their heavy load.

Wrestling the cutting edge of plastic bags
mothers carry goods for all their sons.
The shining ones are hiding out in posh hotels.
A scene that's much the same as Betjeman's.

Victoria is set in bronze and not amused,
unflattered by a wall of Cola lights.
Market stalls are choking her with trinketry,
a carousel rides horses through her nights.

I sit al-freezin'-fresco here, outside the café,
from sticky buns scrape off an icing's sheen,
numbly watch the shoppers shop until they drop,
a merry go, go round; a city scene.

## Found in a Library

In a bulletin:
a miserable child is searching for food;
his ambition's an ordinary life.

On a poster,
on the wall,
someone's friend
tells us he makes rainbows,
a wiseman asks, 'Can you see beyond the horizons?'

There's an inner truth on the inner pages
of the 'Inner Voice' in an inner room
in a Library:

'We are paying too much for life insurance.'

### A Tesco Villanelle
*(for Artsfest)*

All you have to do is smile, say cheese.
Give out sample words for them to try.
You'll find promoting poetry's a breeze.

You know that all the people you can't please.
Some will pick and mix, but some will buy.
All you have to do is smile, say cheese.

Don't worry if their eyes are frozen peas
that they roll around their sockets as they sigh.
Promoting poetry will be a breeze.

Tell them of the free activities;
the Artsfest fun. Don't let it pass them by.
All you have to do is smile, say cheese.

It might sound sausage forced, but I don't tease.
Why do you ask me if a pig can fly?
You'll find promoting poetry's a breeze.

A Tesco villanelle would be quite nice, if you could squeeze
A little one out of your pen... do try.
(I did. And here it is. It smiles...says cheese.
Promoting poetry is such a breeze.)

# A Little Dialectic Please
### (A Riposte)

Where did the bright British go?
Perhaps they're all in hiding,
wondering how to grow an Eden tree
from all the pain you dig up on this page.
This school anthology it scares me, Merle.

Turn history to herstory and right the wrongs of slavery.
When I think of ancient clans, my ancestors; I too could rage.

Shame upon the longboat crew and centuries of centurians who took
their poor barbarians to bed.

Shame upon Victorians, the masters of their house whose chattled
birdsongs gilded tiny cages.

In a bardic cave that is my home a voice in me cries out alone,
'Where are the Celtic names I own? Where do the old ghosts walk?'

A mouth extends a Munchian scream, a dreamer poet dreams a dream.
When words are raw and sharp and mean it does no good to talk.

When all is sad and done, Merle. When all is said and Donne,
we are one continent; a part of all the people we have met.

I hear the clichéd bell that tolls your pain; it tolled mine too.
But is that feeling 'Art'?

In your competition
*Day was looking for poetry of worth*
*for a writing that could wrap up a feelin'*
*an fling it back hard.*

In another competition:
they were looking for poetry of worth,
a writing of place and time.
But when Art is judged politically,
where issues hold a hidden key,
there is no space for folk like we
in the deep spaces,
behind their watching faces,
behind their judging eyes.

I could wrap your anger
*Roun' we little finger*
Add it to *we own*
turn it into something green
that bursts its shirt.

But that is not the Bardic way:
not Art, not life, not me.

*Ah wonder where is de bright British?*
Rhetorically, your question hangs in air.

They found another place to hide
not dialectic diatribe wrapped in a school anthology
where words are probes and thought-screams urge us:
wider,wider, w i d e …until the heads of children
fall apart.

Would you listen to their answer if you heard
the heave-ho pulling of their voices as they row
to beat the drumming of their heart?

I do not know the circled fairy places,
for generations' scissors cut my Gaelic memory.
But I will speak, for I was working class
and in a council house
I grew this tongue
to talk.

They tell me that my being is something simply bound,
a thing that rhymes with farce.
They call me 'woman' 'white' and 'middle class'.

They pickle us in brine and think us tinned,
labelled on a shelf and out of reach,
but only their perceptions form the brand.

We are what we are now.

When your descendants take a foreign map
and look to find Grenada, Trinidad,
do not turn your body in its grave.
Or, if you must, then turn and turn again.

Turn back to where we were one family,
that cradle of humanity:
that space, that distant place, that human tribe.

Be kind.
Be kin.
Be kind.

## *Say it as it is*


'I say it as it is,' she says,
'I call a spade a spade.'

*And then she opens up her mouth and hurtles a grenade.*

'I say it as it is,' she says,
'I say it all by rote.'

*She finds another victim and she grabs them by the throat.*

'I say it as it is,' she says,
'I never bite my tongue,'

*But all of us, just like this line, are destined to be wrong.*

'Its not that I'm irrational
or spoiling for a fight.'

*It's just that we are always wrong and she is always right.*

### Call Down the Colours

Call down the colours
seal her in gold
bring down the light
guard and enfold
her with light
love and calm.
Tell her she's warm
sheltered from harm.
Call down the strength
of the light
that will arm her
and keep out the night;
centre her white.


Cover her gold
and call on the light.
Keep out the pain
of the room that is cold.
Her strength is in violet
her refuge is gold.


Call on the rainbow
call down the star
channel the power
of the light from afar.
Be strong in the calling
and make her to rise
from a bed that lies
far from her far away eyes.

Chisel her granite
drill through her steel.
Pull down the light
and remind her to feel
for the truth of the colour
the hue and the tone,
the seed of her strength
that is calling her home.


Let acceptance and knowledge
Bring strength for the fight.
Centre her white.


Her gift lies in violet's intuitive ray
the cure is within her
and growing each day.


When strength is depleted
the mind cannot hold
its balance from tilting.
Cover her gold.


Safe in the warm
protected from cold
love strengthens within her.
Cover her gold.

## Cricceth
*(A Weekend in Wales)*


No stars to view, just cars, more cars
and traffic cones, then roundabouts,
a crescent moon, a journey out,
speed camera checks, long carriageways
that measure out an English mile,
that measure out an English mile.

A star, a star,
that calls you on
then lanes weave out a long Welsh mile.
They reel us in and wind us out a long Welsh mile.

*Araf, Araf,*
Slow down
Slow down.

*Araf, Araf,*
Slow down.

*Araf, Araf,*
Slow down
Slow down.

A long Welsh mile.

Beside the road, beyond the trees,
the mountains crouch, *the mountains crouch,*
and scores of stars are shining out a long Welsh mile.

*Araf, Araf,*
Slow down
Slow down.

*Araf, Araf,*
Slow down.

*Araf, Araf,*
Slow down
Slow down.

A long Welsh Mile.


On spotlit walls the cars play on
the grey stones dance
*the grey stones dance.*

*Afon y pont*
*Afon y pont*
A long Welsh mile.

*Araf, Araf,*
the signs all say.

*Araf, Araf,*
Slow down.

*Araf, Araf,*
Slow down,
Slow down.
A long Welsh mile.

Arbour trees are framing road
with ancient boughs
*with ancient boughs.*

A nave of wood is rising up
above the road
*above the road*

to weave us through cathedral nights,
to weave us in and weave us out
*a long Welsh night.*

Above our heads are stretching out
scores and scores of starry lights.

On bumpy lane, through farmer's gate
the last long mile is rolling out a journey long
a barred back door that greets us; then a wall to climb.
The torch we brought lights up the steps.
We trip and fall and carry bags.

A river calls
*or is it sea?*
A river calls
*or is it sea?*

Have they forgotten that we come?
Did they forget our journey out?
The night is dark and we are cold.
*A long Welsh mile.*

We bend to find a hidden key
then stretch our eyes to find the stars.

*Y Dryll, Y Dryll.*

The long Welsh mile has brought us to a dolphin view
where choirs of stars spread out to sing a chorus of
a Welsh miled light.
And in the morning, sun rained sea,
a sounding waterfall on stone.
Boulder guards that stand and wait
as muses sing and gulls in air
hold back their breath,
cry not too much
and fly the wind of morning light.

*Y Dryll, Y Dryll.*

The waves are rippling through glass
an inky white on paper beds that spreads itself
to form itself.

A dolphin leaps and we are sea,
an inky pen that rises up and flows us out
a long Welsh night.

*We float upon the surface of the Welsh miled light.*

And you, my daughter, wish a flute into your hands
so you can stand and play the rocks an echo too ethereal
for words to catch, for songs to sing, or crawling cars
to carry back.

With us there is no need to speak,
to pave a mile with ancient words.
You hear the hedge cliff walk that calls

*'To Criccieth. To Criccieth.'*

We share a hug of gentle light and then you leave
to walk the stones, to find the spiralled shell that spins you
through the cradle song of day,

*Y Dryll Y Dryll.*

We are the sea, the sun, the light,
the shining doves that dive to sea,
a choir of voiceless silver wings,
a flickering of light.


A gentle fingered 'Yesterday'
Ripples through the cottage walls,
steps out notes that bring me back
where people talk, a guitar plays,
and someone hums a melody.

Soon we weave our way again through moon and stars
to journey home.
But we have seen the moon in day upon a blue
and sun blessed sky.

A Cymru night in Cymru day
where journey knows no distance.

### *Without Reason*

With feather pillow for her head
she dreamt the dream of those who grow,
when from the bathroom came a thud
that dealt her dragon one last blow.

She never heard the car arrive,
she never heard the siren call.
She only heard her mother's cry
and stifled whispers climb the wall.

## *On Such a Night*

The player plays the bass
she plays the bass

echoes back the echo of a bang

beats to feel the white noise hanging space
taps the geiger counting out of clicks
rides upon the waves that silence swells
between each click…each click…
each tiny click.

'In such a night Troilus methinks
mounted Trojan walls and sighed
his soul towards that Grecian tent
where Cressid lay.'

In such a night did Dido beat her breast
and taking up a willow in her hand
waft her love to come again
to Carthage.

On such a night did this young man
stare upon the Guinness black of night
and wonder at the movement of the stars,
on such a night.

Behind the bar a barman rings the change
pours a pint to make a young man smile.
Sliding down the black silk of a pint
a young man sips his way into the night.
On such a night.

'How far that little candle throws its beams'
Words he heard inside an ancient play
as on the stage a candle shed its light.
Words, when young, he did not understand
and yet they echo through the years tonight.

A Candle
empty bottle
tears of wax
picked and flicked
out on a table top.
His fingers move
he drinks another pint
and wonders why he thinks of plays tonight.

The bass drum beats a pulse to fill his veins
inside his ears he hears a hammer bang,
his stomach turns and churns
resonates the E note of a clarinet
a roller coaster sound that rolls him out
pulls him through the long elastic scales
that rise and fall and rise
and turn and fall.

There was a saxophone, there was a sax,
a player who caressed, undressed
each note.

There was a Cressid once,
a Juliet.
There was a ball where he could wear no mask.

The fingers on the clarinet now rise
marking out the mercury of night.

The player plays the bass,
he plays the bass.

A drummer beats the white noise
hanging space.

A hand wipes off a creamy white moustache.
A hand puts down another empty glass,
another hand puts down an empty glass.

The glass collector adds them to his tray,
the barman empties ashtrays,
waves them with a wiping cloth.

No one sees the nub end of the last lit
unsmoked cigarette when gravity
takes down a line of ash.

On such a night did Thersites
release that puss which festered his vile spot.

On such a night
the player plays the bass.

On such a night the drummer
beats a drum.

on such a night as this,
on such a night.

## *Aurano*

As we rattle the roar of the great thundermouth
watch lightning flash forward the mountains,
in your eyes, there is sea in your eyes
and I think, for a moment, I'm home.

In your halo of arms, in this last cigarette,
in the heap of familiar junk by the bed,
a faithful old slipper with grey bearded head,
for a moment, I think I am home.

Pyracanthus grows up like a fortress with thorns
and wisteria carves down her water on walls,
through the caves of my nostrils a memory calls
and I think for a moment I'm home:

where the eye of the fish swims so close to the bed,
through the skull bone of dreams weave the dreams
of the dead.
In the sea there are fish, in the fish sea is fed
through a silvering body that fountains.

We are here, for a while, half forgetful-awake
to the peace that was ours. This Italian lake
holds the silence of peaks and the cricketing wake
of our senses.

In the lightning that strikes
from the great thundermouth,
in the waterfall rain
in the steam of the trees,
in the opening eye of the fish
and the seas, I will swim
in your eyes. In your eyes.

## Cotswold Stone

Shuffling my feet for warmth to feel my feet
my shoe sends on its journey one small stone.
It flies off to a gate, through arch of greenery
to fields of sun and sheep. I stand alone

beneath this fragile snap of lichened arches,
before the skin of moss that warms a wall
where trinities of leaves weave through a wooden bench
to cover splintered legs with ivyfall.

I move upon a cloak of berries, fallen leaves
to creep between the elder. As I walk
I feel the phantom of a kiss upon my cheek
as wind that sounds as water tries to talk.

## To George Gordon, Lord Byron

Sir,

I hear
you told men of a pleasure,
a pleasure to be found in pathless woods.

I also hear
this crunching gravel path,
the path in this small garden
where I walk.

It too
speaks joy.

### Sonnet of a Staple Diet

The food of love is not a vindaloo
That's spicy hot and taken with a beer,
A truffle rare, champagne sipped from a shoe,
a birthday cake that comes but once a year.

You never were a Chinese take away,
a dial a pizza, plate of fish and chips.
You'd drive out of a drive-in straight away,
a breakfast bar would never pass your lips.

Shall I compare you to Bucks Fizz at dawn,
a chestnut roasted on a Christmas fire,
a jug of Pimms partaken on the lawn,
a grape peeled to the sounding of a lyre.

Love proves itself through years' uncertainty.
You are my clichéd end… my cup of tea.

## A Cup for the World

In the greeting eyes of children born in oriental places
*this day our cup is full*
In the trooping of their colours, in their smiling hearts and faces
*this day our cup is full*

In the rising of a ball that kicks the pathway of a prayer
In the arcing hope of covenant that rainbows through the air
*this day our cup is full*

In the resonating drumming of a stadium of feet
In the rising of an awe that pulls a people from its seat
*this day our cup is full*

In a karaoke Japanese-Korean sing-a-long
In a vindaloo of chanting, in the la la of a song
*this day our cup is full*

In the Knights of St George voices, in the hearts that raise a cheer
as we smite the Bulldog-Dragon with a univocal spear
*this day our cup is full*

When a captain's comrade spirit hugs the anger from his friend
As win or lose the game leads us to honour in the end
*this day our cup is full.*

### Lemon Meringue Pie
*(For Hilary)*


She cracks the egg but never breaks the yolk
yo-yos yellow worlds between her hands.
A hen is just an egg becoming egg
she knows that now and so she
whisks up whiteness into froth
sugar whitens worlds of light meringue
feeds them spoons of sliding apple snow
whisks up mountains, raises them to peaks
and gently folds them out of clinging bowls.
Smiles to see the sweet unconquered peaks
on lemon land that they have made their own.
The yolk she blended in has bound the crumbs:
A base baked blindly, not so blindly baked.

## Sheltered

If you ask her how she is, she will tell you she's okay
she's learnt how to suppress the inner groaning.
He has so many things to do; has such a busy day,
he hasn't time to listen to her moaning.
She tells him, 'Yes, the window box is lovely. Thank you, dear.
It's been watered three times daily since you bought it me last year
by the angels who pop in and out. They've put your favourite beer
in the fridge. Well, just in case. Thank you for phoning.'

No, she doesn't want to move into a home, she says, not yet,
she can manage with the people from the social.
She would like to make him happy; worry less. Does he forget
that her words get all mixed up when she's emotial.
When he says he has to go, she wonders when he'll call again,
takes her water tablets, pressure tablets, ones to numb the pain.
As the window box is drowning in a downpour of the rain
the conundrum of her brain's gone all emotial.

## A Christmas Universe
*(To Charlotte)*

This year you've grown too old for anagrams,
that devil's name within a Santa hat.
You tell me that you have no need of things
or wishes that you'll later learn to curse:
the Midas touch, the genii trickster's lamp
are all behind you.

Oranges, or nuts that you can crack,
chocolate in a stocking by the fire
that you can race to eat before it melts,
that you can suck before the juice runs dry,
that you can squeeze to crack, to break the shell.
A tiny space, a place before the fire,
to have in any order you desire.
It's all you ask.

We sit here, Boxing Day, pyjama clad,
honour silence, nurse a Christmas cold.
Inside our hamlet there's a universe,
a tardis world that grows in cottage walls
where dreams are birthsongs dancing out a flame,
licking coal to life.

*Your brother's reading Feynman on the floor,*
*'You think you'll understand it, but you don't.'*

*A comment ricocheted, it's dad's aside,*
*'You think you'll understand it, but you won't.'*

You sit squashed up with Tigger on a seat,
read 'Lord of the Rings' time and again.
And in his head your Tigger softly says,
'At fifteen years my friend still loves to bounce.
She springs from tale to tale, from spring
to spring.'

I'm curled up in an armchair with this book
writing out a story for myself, feeling like the Pooh-bear
with no brain. Wondering how P-branes intersect to form black
holes.
My thoughts are Christmas ribbons tied in knots, discarded labels
from the day before, hiding in a black bag by the door.
I tap, unwrap a chocolate from its box,
so we can suck each segment
and not speak.

We wonder why the gentle snowflake falls,
solves, dissolves its secrets on our tongues:

*Put a mirror in the middle of the water in the walls,*
*the Christmas birth canal is much too thin a line to carry us.*

Some nuts, its seems, are much too tough to crack
in the small time we are lent in holidays.

## Le Beau Monde

From the punnet of the cradle
to the Graves upon the table
the people who are beautiful
believe they're being fair.
From the savour of a wish,
in the cut glass of a dish,
in the sorbet smear of napkins
to the speech that says they care.

In their symmetry of faces
in the blushing grace of races
from their feet spread out horizons
royal carpets set to deal
up and open doors before them
crowds who worship and adore them.
They're walking in the strawberry fields
of high cheek bone appeal.

From the punnet of the cradle
to the Graves upon the table
inside those strawberry fields
where nothing's really real
there's a Beatle song still singing
there's a wing of chaos ringing
from those butterfly designers
as they flit from deal to deal.

In the cemetery of faces,
in the slowing down of paces
silver service, silver spoon
turns too soon to silver hair.
Time makes fools of all of us
the passion, pear and paw of us
the ugli and the strawberry fruit,
are berried Winter fayre.

## Caterpillars

Lying on the grass to conjure sky
I make a foreman's helmet of a cloud,
feel the sun that burns upon my face,
watch the tiny movement of the grass
creep its small apologies.

Soon the sun moves on and shadows fall.
My body rises up to go inside,
leaves behind my weight of form on grass
as mighty engines make their way back home,
chasing down the motorway they build.

All morning they were moving out like ants;
Metal, shining, blinding things that danced
their bulk of bodies on a hill:
weaving an unspoken winding path,
flashing out the amber of their eyes,

lumbering a way through hollowed ground,
rising after dawn in chorused bleeps,
breaking through the casement of their caul,
digging down the duck down of my sleep
to shift a dreaming soil.

Through August heat and melting afternoons
the monster diggers dig.
They dig down,
deep.

## Mrs Muffin's Tea Shop

Beneath a Ledbury tinted parasol
we listen to a literary voice
pick out raisins, deconstruct a cake.

Did Mrs Muffin breathe a Malvern air,
did she invent these recipes they bake?
Is she inside a corner, cobweb veiled?

Someone jokes that she's a mummy now
her epitaph is in this food they make.
Another says she never was at all.

We drink our fill; a coffee cloud of air
that caffeine pumps us up until we rise
to walk that small stone way to Burgage Hall

where we are ushered in a little late
to slip like ghosts into a strange debate.

## *Free Rider*

He's polishing his face inside the chrome.
He's tightening the wing nuts on the body of his motorbike.
He does the macho man thing on his own,
travels without donkey, rides alone.

He cuts the mother cord, turns off the phone,
claps one hand to catch the wind that spirits through the motorbike.
He watches clouds fly out through silver foam
as signposts take him out and  bring him home.

## Snowhill to Priestfields

*'Somewhere on the seven Roman hills*
*the gods rolled down another soul to life.'*
The first trip we took out was from Snowhill.
We took a tram too soon, they called us back
and so we left that tram and crossed the track
admired the snow scene etchings in a shelter
at St Paul's and waited for a tram
to take us back.

*'Somewhere on these seven Brummie hills*
*the gods roll down a soul again to life.'*
The second time we took the journey out
my mind remembered Antioch, Iconium.
We stopped to rest a while in Hockley's sigh
and walked as tourists through the gems of streets
where Dad's three elder brothers had been born.

Now painted cardboard takes the place of glass
and strong portcullis padlocked gates on doors
protect the old illusions.

*'Somewhere on those far Olympian hills*
*they drank the golden nectar of a truth*
*and watched the souls that struggled out a life.'*
When we next stepped upon a tram again
I journeyed in and out of time and thought
sought to find my bearings in a sign.

Then came the pink lit shrubs of Benson Road
where shoes turned ruby slippers
moved to dance the yellow winding of the rails.

*'Far away from far Olympian hills*
*they look for signs to find where they began*
*search to find the route that takes them back.'*
At Hawthorns, while exhaling breath on glass,
I tried to draw the glass etched snowy hills
caught and carved on shelters near the track,
wondered at the blue line of a bannister
bound by golden rails on either side.

By 'Trinity' there were no subtle signs
just Monty Python feet that stomped in air;
a crowish vision of a childhood priest
who rode his whiplash tongue upon a bike
to rule his parish in an Irish brogue:

*'Catholic girls belong in Catholic schools.*

*..in nomine Patri et filii et spiritus sancti...'*

'At Priestfields this tram terminates.'

*'Amen.'*

The first trip that we took was from Snowhill.
We learnt to ski off piste and push back air
but somewhere on the blue course of the trails
a simple slip, a signal brought us back.

The second time we moved much further out
but never reached those Wolverhampton sights.
I wondered if there really was an Oz,
a wizard at the end of yellow rails,
why tunnels measure time as we move back,
if somewhere on those far Elysian hills,
if somewhere on the apres ski of heights
gods enjoy the nectar taste of sky.

*'Behind us all there stands a snowy hill,*
*a silver tray that slides us down a slope,*
*a snowball fall of children pushing air.'*

## *Mitochondrial Eve*

We walk to the valley of the moon.
We drink from the waters that run free.
We listen to the voices of our ancestors.
We are one people…

We walk to the valley of the moon.
We drink from the waters that run free.
We listen to the voices of our ancestors.
We are one people…

We walk to the valley of the moon.
We drink from the waters that run free.
We listen to the voices of our ancestors.
We are one people…

Family.

# GLOSSARY

**Chant** Verses that are celebrated, sung or intoned, primal chants from around the world. They can be performed with musical instruments, recited as a chorus and choreographed with movement. Vowel sounds follow Bardic traditions to create resonance and rhythm; repetition of the verse moves to unite the voices of the tribe. (eg *Mitochondrial Eve*)

**Epitaph** Serious or humorous short verse on tombstone to commemorate the person buried there. (eg *Birmingham Rhapsody: 'Here lies Jane...'*)

**Found** 'Extraction' and 'context' are the key words. *Found in a Library* was found as the title indicates. Discover your own found-poem by looking around and paying attention to the details in the local environment.

**Ghazal** The Moorish form is a fourteen line ode, often a love song. The Persian and Arabic form is made up of a selection of couplets. The first two lines and after that, all even numbered lines, rhyme.
Urdu ghazals sound poignant and powerful. The subject matter is often spiritual or romantic, and commonly a phrase is repeated at the end of the first two lines and then at the end of each even line which forms the final line of each successive couplet. Due to space this phrase had to be set out on a separate line in this book. (eg *A Cup for the World*)

**Haiku** Japanese form of seventeen syllables arranged in three lines of five, seven and five syllables. One is found in the *Birmingham Rhapsody* and starts: *'See the Smartie car.* Traditional forms contain a 'kigo' which names or alludes to one of the four seasons. My haiku uses 'spring' to show the movement of the car. A 'Renga' is a longer poem beginning with a haiku.

**Mock Heroic** Writing about trivialities in a highbrow style. The opening invocation of *Birmingham Rhapsody: 'Of man's own rising...pantomime'* also parodies the opening of Milton's epic poem *Paradise Lost*.

**Pantoum** In a Pantoum the second and fourth line of each stanza become the first and third of the next stanza...eventually the *a* rhyme of the first verse is reached again in the last stanza. (eg *Loading the Glass Washer*)

**Parody** An attempt to make fun of a particular author or style by close copying. *Birmingham Rhapsody: 'Lift not your fist against the Hyatt*

*Tower'* refers back to Milton's Sonnet VIII: '*Lift not thy spear against the Muses' bower.'*

**Performance** Performance pieces were often composed specifically for performance and this is evident in the language. Many raps are satirical or political, full of emotion. Some performance pieces are lyrical. Jazzoetry comes alive with a jazz band. Some poems work in performance but not on the page, others manage to work in both situations. The following poems have a performance element: *Birmingham Rhapsody, Metro Motion, A Little Dialectic Please, Call Down the Colours, On Such a Night, Aurano, From Snowhill to Priestfields.*

**Rap** A strong rhythmic beat, often spoken to music. Sometimes rhyming couplets are used; sometimes alternate rhyming and sometimes, none. There is often a strong rhyme but it is the powerful rhythm that must be evident. (eg *Birmingham Rhapsody: The Jerk in the Merc, Itta Rap.*)

**Riposte** I have used this term to describe *A Little Dialectic Please* because it is, in essence, a reply to the poem *No Dialects Please* by Merle Collins (2002 OCR school poetry anthology).

**Rondel** A lyric poem of thirteen or fourteen lines. A Rondel had two rhymes usually rhymed *abba abab abb aab* but there are other variations. (eg *Essentials* and *Atonement)*

**Sestina** Six six-lined stanzas are followed by a three line stanza. The end words of the six lines are rearranged on a different line in each of the first six verses. The final three line verse includes the other end words in the middle of the line. *Memories in a City Café* is a rhymed sestina with an elongated ending to stress the eternal nagging of the wife.

**Sonnet** The sonnet has a number of forms but the one included in this book is the popular Shakespearean sonnet of fourteen lines grouped *abab, cdcd, efef, gg.* (eg *Sonnet of a Staple Diet)*

**Triolet** Eight line verse, the first line is repeated on the fourth and seventh line and the second line is repeated on the last line. The rhyming scheme is *abaaabab.* (eg *The Lady in Red*)

**Villanelle** Five tercets are followed by a quatrain: *A(1)- b- A(2), a- b-A(1), a-b-A(2), a-b-A(1), a-b-A(2), abA(1)A(2).* (eg *Tesco Villanelle*)

# Biography

Born Julie Davis, in Sutton Coldfield, England, in 1960. Julie has lived in the West Midlands region for all of her life. From the early 1980s to the early noughties she lived at Moxhull Hall Hotel with her husband John and their children, Nathaniel and Charlotte. Whilst bringing up their young family she opened a Nursery School in the old Chauffeur's cottage where, after a later conversion, the family lived for many years.

Julie worked as a teacher, special needs advisor and creative advisor to schools. She co-directed *Poetry Pals* and during her year as Birmingham Poet Laureate in 2002-2003, founded the *Oasis Café Theatre*. Thanks to a grant from the Arts Council she co-founded and directed *Poetry Central*. She continues to travel nationally and internationally as a poet in order to conduct workshops and masterclasses, judge competitions, give readings and perform poetry. Julie mentors emerging poets, tutors on residential poetry workshops, runs In-set for teachers and lecturers of English.

Julie is currently Poet in Residence at Symphony Hall, Birmingham. Occasionally she has been afforded such luxuries as a fellowship at *Hawthornden Castle* where she she is able to retreat from the busy world awhile in order to write.

# Acknowledgements

Apart from - as always - my family, there are many friends, other artists and specific groups to thank. I am sorry I cannot name everyone here...but thank you.
Thanks must also go to a battered bag that was lost, found again and led me to Brian who has been an honest critic, a rigorous editor and a dear friend. Many thanks to Reini for her eagle eyed expertise and patience, to Harry for the cover - and the chips, to Helena for her warmth of hospitality, her friendship and advice, and to Jonathan Davidson for agreeing to write the preface. Thank you.